CROWNS
OF HEBRON

A DAVID STORY BOOK 1

NICHOLAS LANGAN ILLUSTRATED BY ANDREW LAITINEN

LUCIDBOOKS

Crowns of Hebron
A David Story
Book 1

Published by Lucid Books in Houston, TX
www.LucidBooksPublishing.com

ISBN-10: 1-63296-327-2
ISBN-13: 978-1-63296-327-7
eISBN-10: 1-63296-329-9
eISBN-13: 978-1-63296-329-1

Special Sales: Most Lucid Books titles are available in special quantity discounts. Custom imprinting or excerpting can also be done to fit special needs. Contact Lucid Books at Info@LucidBooksPublishing.com.

Special thanks to God for bringing me onto this spinning rock and keeping me alive once here; to my parents for encouraging creativity; to my children for keeping me young; to Scott and Tyler for listening to my crazy ideas and telling me when something was no good; and to Kasey for pushing me to work hard and take risks in order to fulfill my crazy dreams.

Characters

KING SAUL

 JONATHAN

GOLIATH

 URIAH

AHIAH

 ELIAB

Late 11th Century BCE

The Israelites, attempting to flourish in a war-torn Promised Land, have received Saul as their first king.

A cautious man, Saul struggles under the enormous weight of attempting to rule justly and keep his people alive.

Saul's son Jonathan, beloved by the men under his command, believes God will grant military victory over the numerically superior Philistines.

Saul is not so sure.

GIBEAH

THE NEXT MORNING

GILGAL

IF MY SON DIES, SO DO YOU.

WHAT WILL HAPPEN NEXT?

CHECK OUT
CROWNS OF HEBRON BOOK 2
TO FIND OUT!

www.ingramcontent.com/pod-product-compliance
Lightning Source LLC
Chambersburg PA
CBHW041436040426

42452CB00024B/2991